Ten *fun* Things to Do Before You Die

Ten fun Things to Do Before You Die

by nun other than
Karol A. Jackowski

AVE MARIA PRESS   Notre Dame, Indiana 46556

First printing, October, 1989
Fourth printing, March, 1994
30,000 copies in print

Illustrations

Page 14   Wanda Wallenda stamp © Ken Brown Stamps, Saxtons River, VT 05154. Used by permission.

Page 33   Non-believer at the beach stamp © Ken Brown Stamps, Saxtons River, VT 05154. Used by permission.

Page 37   Jane Wagner, *The Search for Signs of Intelligent Life in the Universe*, New York: Harper & Row, 1986, 18.

Page 47   Stamps #1, #3 and #5 © Ken Brown Stamps, Saxtons River, VT 05154. Used by permission.

Page 51   Etty Hillesum, *An Interrupted Life*, New York: Washington Square Press, 1981, 124.

Page 82   *The Collected Works of St. John of the Cross*, Kieran Kavanaugh, O.C.D. and Otilio Rodriguez, O.C.D., trans., Washington, D.C.: ICS Publications, 1973, 543.

Page 85   *An Interrupted Life*, 26-28.

Pages 96-97   Anne Bancroft, *Origins of the Sacred*, London, New York: Arkana, 1987, 54. Swimmer and monster stamps © Ken Brown Stamps, Saxtons River, VT 05154. Used by permission.

Page 103   *The Collected Works of St. John of the Cross*, 519-520.

Unless otherwise indicated, scripture quotations used in this work are taken from THE NEW JERUSALEM BIBLE, copyright © 1985 by Darton Longman & Todd, Ltd. and Doubleday & Co., a division of the Bantam Doubleday Dell Publishing Group. All rights reserved. Used with permission of the publisher.

International Standard Book Number: 0-87793-409-6

Library of Congress Catalog Card Number: 89-84558

Cover and text design by Katherine Robinson Coleman.

Printed and bound in the United States of America.

This book is dedicated
with endless love
to my very best friend
in the whole world

_____.

Ten *fun* Things to Do Before You Die

Foreword

In its original form, this book was a lecture given in the spring of 1987 at Saint Mary's College, Notre Dame, Indiana. As part of a student-planned program called "The Last Lecture Series," invitees were asked to prepare a lecture pretending it was the last one given before they died—their parting words.

Lecturing has never been one of my burning interests; making lists, on the other hand, is a source of great fascination for me, and obviously for countless others (e.g., The Ten Commandments, 50 Ways to Leave Your Lover, The Seven Deadly Sins). Lists. Making a list of all the things I'm glad I did before I die, and all the things I highly recommend that others think about doing before they die, is how this book got started. The list turned into a lecture, which then looked like an outline for a book, the end result of which you are holding in your hands.

One thing to know about this particular list is that the items are not given in any order of importance. I've simply put them down in the way they came to mind. All have been profoundly important at one time or another, and some all the time. So don't be shocked to find that, for a nun, fun is number one on the list and God number three. All ten things connect. None stands alone or apart from the others.

Making your own list is a must. The experience itself is worth tons more than the price of this book. Plus you never know for sure what will happen. "Ten More (fun) Things to Do Before You Die" has a nice ring to it. Or "Ten Things Never to Do Before You Die." Ask children to make a list. I asked my sister's kids (Jon 10, Ellen 7 and Matt 5) what one thing they thought everybody should do before they die. Immediately and with great enthusiasm all three yelled, "Watch G.L.O.W. on Saturday night" (G.L.O.W. Gorgeous Ladies of Wrestling). Then came their list of favorite G.L.O.W. girls—Tina Ferrari, Mountain Fiji, Attache, Palestina and Soul Patrol. My favorite was the tag team of Spike and Chainsaw.

Obviously the possibilities are endless and fun. Do make your own list.

TEN THINGS TO DO BEFORE YOU DIE

1.
2.
3.
4.
5.
6.
7.
8.
9.
10.

First Thing:

Have More Fun Than Anyone Else

Having more fun than anyone else is the very first thing to do before you die. Fun—my favorite F-word. While having more fun than anyone else means you'll have to work twice as hard for not appearing to be serious, it's well worth the extra effort. Nothing refreshes, comforts and soothes weary souls like a good time. Nothing exhilarates and sends the spirit soaring more than having the best time ever. With an infinite number of ways to have more fun than anyone else, it took me 42 years to find four:

    1. *Find Fun People*

One of the hardest things to find in life is fun people. Far too few appear and seemingly fewer survive adulthood. While it's certainly possible and admirable to have more fun than anyone else when you're alone, the pure joy of fun is more often than not multiplied and intensified by the company of other fun people.

In the serious search for fun people, these are some things to watch for: good storytelling, perfect timing, interesting work, a good appetite, unusual sense of humor, fresh insight, and a brave daring life. Finding fun people for the rest of your life is a sure guarantee for having more fun than anyone else. For that reason alone, it's most preferable to do *before* you die, not after.

2. *Don't Think About Yourself
    Around Other People*

There are people in life who lack the desire to raise their spirit and conversation above themselves. That is near irremediable. Thinking and talking only about yourself when around others is tiresome, boring, and the number one killer of fun. Most importantly, thinking and talking only about yourself render you incapable of having more fun than anyone else.

A good general rule is to think about yourself when you're by yourself and, in the presence of others, think and ask about them. Expressing interest in the life and work of those around you not only bestows a delightful reputation of being an interesting person and good conversationalist, but also reveals in short order the persons with the most activated potential for fun. So whatever you do, forget about yourself around other people. Not to do so is also just plain rude.

3. *Be a Fun Person*

The surest way to have more fun than anyone else is for you yourself to be a fun person. Usually, where there is no fun, put fun and you will find fun. Occasionally you will also find furrowed brows and

BEING
A
FUN
PERSON
IS THE
HALLMARK
OF
TRUE MATURITY.

WANDA
WALLENDA

disapproving eyes—but never mind. That too is near irremediable.

There are two big parts to being a fun person. One is to make yourself interesting and the other has to do with perfect timing. Making yourself interesting proves so important to being a fun person that it turned up as the seventh thing to do before you die, thus warranting its own chapter.

Perfect timing is a whole other matter and has to do with paying careful attention to the events of the day as they happen, watching all the time for opportunities that have potential for great fun (e.g., Clyde Peeling's Reptile Farm off the Pennsylvania Turnpike, any Dairy Queen, and boring yes boring meetings). There is no time with more divine potential for fun than the present moment. You get it once and never again. So pay extra attention to the strange, disturbing, boring, moving and hilarious events of the day—the high energy centers where potential for relief and release is greatest. A fun person is forever watchful of the perfect moment and rarely fails to seize it.

4.   *If It Looks Like Fun and Doesn't*
     Break the Ten Commandments, Do It

Limitations may seem distasteful and confining, but they have (without fail) proven to be indescribably essential to my having more fun than anyone else: limits, boundaries, knowing when to stop, the line beyond which we do not go without hurting or getting hurt.

Pursuing unlimited possibilities does little more than overwhelm us with countless experiences which move faster than our conscious selves can keep up with. Without limitations we gradually go crazy,

16

become more automatic and more impulsive, losing the spontaneity, freshness and delight which characterize the clear pure vision of the mind's eye. Before long, the juggling act of unlimited possibilities falls apart, and a dizzy confusing unrest becomes a way of life. Getting thrown off balance, we end up shifting priorities, consequently knowing ourselves, others and God less and less. Never a very pretty picture.

Limitations are designed to keep us from destroying life in the endless pursuit of happiness. Without a few basic guidelines for enjoyable living, the capacity to get lost, seriously hurt or killed, greatly magnifies. For nuns, and others like them in this regard, the gospel is the rule of life. Then always we have the Ten Commandments, probably the most famous and reliable set of rules we know. There are others. In just thinking for a short time I came up with seven more commandments.

Nobody likes rules for living very much because they are usually too hard to follow, and more often than not appear to stand in the way of a really good time. Nonetheless, you are not at all likely to have more fun than anyone else without them. So if it looks like fun and doesn't break the Ten Commandments, do it.

SEVEN MORE COMMANDMENTS

 WORK HARD. BUT NOT CONSTANTLY TOO HARD.

 DON'T LIE.

 TRY NOT TO HURT ANYONE.

 BEFRIEND THE ENEMY.

 MODERATION IN ALL THINGS. INCLUDING MODERATION.

 NEVER GET INTO A SPITTING CONTEST WITH A SKUNK

 KNOW THYSELF.

Second Thing:

Get Some Insight

Without insight it's nearly impossible to have more fun than anyone else. Getting insight means finding your very best self and being wowed by the discovery. The starting point is the self. Be prepared for a breathtaking experience. Seeing how you really and truly are oftentimes leaves too much or too little air to breathe.

There is nothing worse than a person with no insight. None more pitiable than the emperor with no clothes. Without insight we're left with an incredible ability to act in purely egotistic and destructive ways, doomed to join the Living Dead or the Stepfords with all of life sucked clean out of them. This is the stuff horror movies are made of. God spare us.

Insight is the most comforting feature of self-knowledge. It usually comes from going through (not ignoring, avoiding or working around) ordinary life events, always trying to be your very best self. Finding your best self and being that person is what happens when you get insight. If you don't find your

own very best self other people will find plenty of
selves for you, and that always has disastrous results,
oftentimes deadly. Starting with wanting to be a better
person, insight gradually goes deeper, moving toward
places of greater compassion, understanding and fun.
Because it saves and nourishes the soul, getting insight
is probably the most important thing to do before you
die. Repeat: Nothing is worse than people with no
insight. All they do is make God want to spit and
vomit (Rv 3:16). So for God's sake and your own,
don't mess around. Find your very best self and be
that person.

Getting Started

Because getting insight has to do with finding your
best self, you will most likely need some kind of
solitude in order to hear yourself think. Some quiet
time alone is a must must must unless you want to be
driven forever by the Seven Deadly Sins, or eaten
alive, or God knows what else. Never a very pretty
picture.

In wondering what to think about with time alone,
start with something like your life and how pleased
you are with the way it's turning out. There's no better
place for getting insight than the ordinary events of life
and what we choose to do with them. In
contemplating life's current condition, think about two
questions: Who is your very best self, and is she or he
alive and well, terminally ill or dead?

1.   *Who is your very best self?*

Thinking about the kind of best self you want to be
is a good place to start getting some insight. The more
specific you are about how you want to be, the greater
the potential for insight. For example, wanting to be a

"nice person" isn't quite as helpful as wanting to be less judgmental of people who do things you don't agree with. For every quality you want in your own very best self, be certain you can see what it might look like in real true life. Name very specific examples of each. Specific is always far more true and interesting than vague.

Making a list right now is a good idea. List the special combination of all the qualities you want in creating a best self, always making sure you can see real true life examples of each. According to Carl Sagan, "We are all made of star stuff." And given that there are 100,000 teenie weenie individual genes that make up every person, the potential list of star stuff is practically endless.

JMJ

MY VERY BEST SELF

1. FUN.

2.

3.

4.

5.

6.

7.

8.

9.

10.

2. *Is your very best self alive and well,*
    terminally ill or dead?

Next, take the "Very Best Self List," check it with your life, and see how close you are to being your best self. The more situations you can find for each item on your list, the stronger that quality is likely to be in you. The fewer situations you can find for each item, the more questionable that quality is likely to be in you.

While viewing all parts of life, pay particular attention to four main areas: important people, important events, major turning points, and consequences of decisions made during important events and major turning points. Heavy! This overall life checkup is the hard-work side of having more fun than anyone else, the side lots of people don't want to bother with because that's where mistakes stay hidden and forever mistaken.

Now in looking at important people, events and major turning points, check to see if you were or are your very best self. If your list of qualities is full of things already working in your life, I'd say you have found your very best self and she or he appears to be alive and well. If on your list you can't find very many of the items at work in your life, that also gives some indication of your current condition: alive, but probably not very well; possibly terminally ill; maybe even given up for dead. A dreadful thought.

Another big place for insight lies in the wild wonderful world of truth or consequences. Truth is what makes you miserable before it sets you free. Consequences are the divinely ingenious full-blown obvious effects of our decisions. Both give the clearest indication of how well we know ourselves and our precious ulterior motives. "If the core of our being is directed to God, then our creative moods, feelings, actions and decisions will bring peace, joy and tranquillity, while the destructive elements within us and outside us will bring agitation, sadness and inner turmoil. If the core of our being is turned away from God, our destructive moods, feelings, actions and decisions will comfort and console us, while the creative elements within us and outside us will trouble and upset us with stings of conscience and remorse."[1] Consequences tell all.

Now take a long steady look at your biggest life decisions and how they turned out. Decisions which survive the ups and downs of life usually come from the very best self, while those which turn out to be troublesome and short-lived usually come from a self which is not altogether the very best. Both eventually yield insight. But the advantage of allowing your very best self to make all decisions comes in getting self-knowledge faster, which brings insight, thus preventing gross stupidity and embarrassing middle-age adolescence.

---

[1]Gerard W. Hughes, *God of Surprises*, Mahway, N.J.: Paulist Press, 1986, p. 93.

One who knows Himself is
STRONGER in knowing than
one who knows His LORd;
and one who is veiled from
Himself is more Heavily veiled
than one who is veiled from
his LORd.

AL-ALAWiU
SUFi SAINT

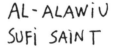

So There.

KAROL JACKOWSKI

Third Thing:

Get Some Depth

If you're having more fun than anyone else and getting some insight, it won't be long before you also acquire some depth. Getting depth is another very important thing to do before you die, especially for nuns. Depth is a big goal for nuns because life as we know it makes no sense without it. Through various forms of sensory deprivation (the three "wows" of poverty, celibacy and obedience) the experience of life (i.e., God) is intensified, which prevents one from becoming a shallow person with nothing more than flesh and blood and nobody home. That's the nun belief.

With insight you find your very best self. With depth you find your very best God. Eventually wisdom comes, embraces you and shows that you both are really one and the same. God abides at home in our very best self and that's what makes us so divine. Every religion from the most primitive to the most contemporary is founded on the belief that being in touch with a god is absolutely necessary.

The most logical way to get depth is to dig for it. Go beyond the obvious to the heart of the matter and see what hidden influences are at work. Those little foxes, the ulterior motives, hide beneath the surface and beg never to see the light of day.

Because the kingdom of God is like a buried treasure (Mt 13:44), there's simply no depth, treasure or God to be found without digging. You can't have clear vision without looking beyond appearances. Digging is what depth is all about: digging until you find buried treasure, maybe even the Holy Grail. Digging and fainting, digging and finding clear cool water, or maybe just digging and getting filthy dirty. No matter the cost, digging in and getting depth moves you closer to the three "very bests": very best self, very best God, and very best creative work ever.

Now in bible stories God hovers anytime there's oppression, death, guilt, suffering, sin or trouble in River City. In the *Book of Job*, God speaks out of a storm, the voice from the whirlwind. The God of the *Bhagavad Gita* is a "shatterer of worlds." The God of Moses is a "consuming fire." You can see when life gets intense so does God—sometimes intensely near, sometimes intensely far, sometimes intensely silent, sometimes bestowing incredible excesses of strength. Sometimes nada nada nada.

Nonetheless, it all goes to show that the very best God is likely to be found in the unknown, unseen, undone parts of life. The parts that hurt, besides making you sick and tired, are the places to dig—places where you've been taken to the limit. Sad

28

but true, the confusing, painful and overwhelming parts of life prove to be excellent starting points for finding out what God will and will not do. Dig in where life lies motionless and at a standstill.

You can take great comfort in knowing that after you handle the painful stuff (the dirt) for a while, it all becomes exceedingly precious. Strange but true; strange because it doesn't make sense; true, because the deeper you go the closer you get to your very best self, your very best God and the very best of everything else in life. To understand fully the depths of pain and joy without being undone or driven crazy by the experience—that's the trick. Some mean trick!

Knowing where to look for God is one thing, but recognizing a very best God when you see one is quite another, and perhaps even more tricky. Here are two more lists to help you recognize God. If your God does and does not do the things on the lists, I'd say you found your very best God. If not, keep digging.

✌ TWO CHECKLISTS ✌

☆ SEVEN THINGS A VERY BEST GOD WILL NOT DO ☆

- ☐ TAKE PAIN AWAY.
- ☐ KILL OR HIT.
- ☐ GIVE UP.
- ☐ BORE YOU OR WASTE YOUR TIME.
- ☐ LIE.
- ☐ LEAVE YOU ALONE,
- ☐ WHATEVER YOU WANT.

I WANT IT.

☆ SEVEN THINGS A VERY BEST GOD WILL DO ☆

☐ MAKE YOU WAIT.

☐ CALM FEARS.

☐ SHOW WHAT TO DO NEXT (EVEN IF NOTHING).

☐ MAKE YOU LAUGH OR BLINK.

☐ GET YOU THROUGH.

☐ MAKE LIFE INTERESTING.

☐ SET YOU FREE.

I LIKE IT.

A Word About Non-Believers

Believers, avid believers, tend to be sinfully judgmental when it comes to the subject of non-believers. Mostly non-believers are those who find that human life itself is divine and that's enough. Or they think life is not divine and that's just the way things are. They say, "That's all there is anyhow so why bother?"

Most non-believers have just never seen what a very good God can do and find it hard to believe such a God exists. Gods who command people to build instead of feed, as well as other gods made in someone else's image and likeness, all warrant nothing but the most profound disbelief. Non-believers have no desire for any of the gods they know and the mere thought of one is oppressive.

Before dogmatism took charge, faith in God meant trusting and experiencing one's own conscience, the gut-feeling intuition, as divine. All of life was believed to be infused and charged with the sacred. Those were the good old days. With the universe as temple, the non-believer can find as many ways to the truth as there are moments in a day. Non-believers firmly believe that one ought not stake absolute claims as to which way of truth is good, better or best. Those categories simply do not apply to divine matters.

Non-believers tend to know mostly who the very best God isn't, and believers tend to know mostly who the very best God is. The truth of the matter is that neither lies very far from the other. Both stand back to back, making a nice balance.

Fourth Thing:

Find a Place to Escape Reality

Well, after coming out of the depths, you can be sure you'll either want to take a long hot tub bubble bath or find another way to escape reality, or both. Escaping reality is the only way not to lose sight of what's Real. It's also one of the best things I learned to do before I die. As a matter of fact, I learned it so soon and so fast it could be inborn. Without places inside and out to escape reality I'm sure I'd be bored to death, sick to death or just plain outright dead.

Knowing limits or being pushed to the ends of them is all it takes to set off the need to escape reality. Because we are not God, the more we exceed our limits, the more we need to escape. Too much limitlessness is just plain too much: overwhelming overload. Enough is enough is enough. No one knows better than you when you've reached or gone past your limit. So, when enough is definitely enough, find a place to escape reality and don't come back until you have to.

WHY ESCAPE
By Jane Wagner

Reality is the leading
cause of stress amongst
those in touch with it.
I can take it in small doses, but
as a lifestyle I found it too confining.
It was just too needful;
it expected me to be there for it
all the time,
and with all I have to do --
I had to let something go.

Now,
since I put reality on a back burner,
my days are jam-packed
and
fun-filled.

Great Escapes: Inside and Out

A. Great Outside Escapes
   1. *Water*

Lakes. Baths. Oceans. Hot tubs. Showers. Nothing comforts, soothes, cleanses and refreshes the weary body and soul like clear cool or hot water. "As the deer yearns for running streams, so I long for you, my God" (Ps 42:1). "By tranquil streams the Shepherd God leads me, to restore my spirit" (Ps 23:2). Water. In the beginning that's all there was: "The earth was a formless void, there was darkness over the deep, with a divine wind sweeping over the waters" (Gn 1:1). Nothing is created and nothing survives without it. Jesus says water is a lot like God. "No one who drinks the water that I shall give will ever be thirsty again: the water that I shall give will become a spring of water, welling up for eternal life" (Jn 4:14).

Divine, God-like water. Holy water charged with the likeness of God. There's no greater comfort to a parched lifeless soul than water: big, everybody's, altogether trustworthy and refreshing. Swimming, fishing, bathing, floating, wading or just sitting nearby resting all feel like sacramental, magic ways to escape reality. Because water is a lot like God, it probably has the greatest potential for a divine escape.

   2. *Exercise*

When it comes to exercise, I do not know whereof I speak. As a firm believer in never running unless someone is chasing me and never buying shoes I have to bend over to tie, I have never found exercise a great escape. When it comes to "No pain, no gain," the thought alone makes me weak. As far as I'm concerned, there's enough pain in life as it is. Why inflict more upon yourself and sometimes others?

For the rest of the world, however, exercise is one of the greatest ways to relieve stress and escape reality. Doctors and health experts everywhere now say you won't live as long without it. The unenlightened prefer to take their chances. Nonetheless, while cultivating a diverse group of friends, I have seen bodies and souls refreshed by spas, aerobics, triathalons, marathons, biking, running, getting bruised and broken in soccer and pumping iron. All of the above fall into the category of things which surpass my understanding. Nevertheless, many fine individuals find exercise a tried and true way to escape reality *and* find rest for the body and soul. I remain unconvinced and overweight.

3. *Travel*

What more obvious way to escape reality than to leave where you are and go somewhere else? Travel near or far. Favorite spots, like all the old familiar places, offer a safe, secure, trustworthy escape. New spots, like places you've never been before, places you've never seen, offer an escape that's more lively, exciting and stimulating. In the end, both provide divine rest and refreshment.

Distance is travel's finest feature. For getting away from it all, sometimes an ocean of distance is necessary, while other times several miles will do. The point is to get as much distance as necessary. The wisdom of the Old Testament teaches that travel and distance add to one's resourcefulness. For the much traveled person who hopes in God, distance is a ". . . mighty shield and strong support, a shelter from the heat, a shade from the noonday sun, a guard against stumbling, a help against falling. It lifts up the spirits, brings a sparkle to the eyes, gives healing, life

earth's crammed with heaven
and every common bush
afire with God;
and only he who sees

takes off his shoes
the rest sit around it
and pluck blackberries.

e.B. Browning

and blessing" (Sir 34:9-17, *NAB*). When reality consistently smothers the life out of you, there's neither a better nor a more fun escape than the blessed distance which travel brings.

B.   Great Inside Escapes

   1.   *Imagination*

Imagination is everyone's inborn place to escape reality. William Blake believed imagination was the "divine body in everyone." Superior devotion to reading is a sure way to cultivate and feed one's imagination. There's nothing quite like picking up a good book and wallowing around in someone else's world for a while. Since most good stories are about the interior of our lives, reading offers a rare and delightful kind of self-knowledge not found in too many other places, besides providing a great escape.

A superior devotion to reading often leads to imagination's other best friend, writing (or any kind of creating, for that matter). Writing is so important to the life of my imagination that it ended up fifth on the list of things to do before I die, demanding its own chapter. Imagination is always closer to us than we are to ourselves. This makes it an escape we can enter into anywhere, anytime, even in the midst of the most boring and unbearable of circumstances. The closest, most convenient, most delightful, most divine and least expensive escape of all is the imagination—and the bigger, the better.

   2.   *Sleep*

Sleep is among my favorite escapes. It is probably the greatest and best healer I know. Sleep brings dreams that can carry us into those divine, mysterious places where rest abides. Rest, one of my favorite activities. When it comes to fears, worries and all

manner of anxieties, there's no greater escape than
sleep.

In a favorite poem, "On Sleep" by Charles Peguy,
God advises

> And I tell you
> Put off until tomorrow
> Those worries and those troubles which are
>   gnawing at you today
> And might very well devour you today. . .
> Put off until tomorrow those tears which
>   fill your eyes and head,
> Flooding you, rolling down your cheeks, those
>   tears which stream down your cheeks.
> Because between now and tomorrow, maybe I,
>   God, will have passed your way. . .
> And I say Blessed, blessed is the man who puts off
>   what he has to do until tomorrow.
> Blessed is he who puts off.
> That is to say Blessed is he who hopes.
> And who sleeps.[1]

If the Catholic church were to add to its list of
sacraments, sleep would be my recommendation for
number eight because sleep always offers what's
needed to get up and begin again.

3. *Retreat*

"Retreat" is a more sanctified word for escaping
reality. The ancient Chinese philosophy of the *I Ching*
says it's the correct way to behave in order not to
exhaust one's forces.[2] When life makes you crazy, the
thing to do is keep still. Withdraw for a while. Wrap
yourself in silence and cordially escape reality. Retreat.
Meditate. Contemplate. Rest.

A source of great inner strength, retreat provides
time for you to catch your breath and swallow your

41

spit (Jb 7:19). Retreating also prevents you from endangering or violating your very best self and your very strongest convictions. The greatest of all escapes lifts you up, gets you through and returns you to life pretty brand new. A good retreat will do that every time.

Being a nun is ideally the greatest of all escapes for women. However, it doesn't take very long to find that, short of major felonies, there's not a whole lot outside the convent that you don't also find inside the convent. It's just controlled better and far more subtle. Which mostly goes to show that you shouldn't worry too much about whether a particular escape is good or not so good. There's no escaping your self and that's all that matters.

In determining how good a particular escape may be, it's all just a matter of time. The trick is to keep an eye on the consequences. Are you better or worse? More truthful or more deceptive? Calmer or more anxious? More accepting or more judgmental? Sicker or healthier? More fun or more boring? Consequences never ever lie.

---

[1]Charles Peguy, God Speaks, New York: Pantheon Books, 1945, p. 30-31.
[2]The I Ching, Richard Wilhelm, trans., Bollingen Series XIX, Princeton, N.J.: Princton University Press, 1977, p. 129.

Fifth Thing:

Write Something at the End of Every Day

For most people, writing something at the end of every day would be one BIG waste on a list of things to do before you die. Most hate to write and are so tired at the end of the day that all they want is a hot tub, a cold drink, to be left alone, to drop dead, or all four. So why write? Why at the end of the day? Why at the end of every day? And what's there to write about anyhow?

Why Write at the End of the Day?

To understand this particular point, you need to know that one of the finest features of nun life was, and for some still is, something called The Great Silence. Grand Silence. Even the name has extra special appeal.

According to monastic tradition, Great Silence was the time from the closing of evening recreation (around 7:30 p.m.), until after meditation the next morning (around 7:30 a.m.). While there was always a general overall nun rule of silence, profound and serious emphasis was given to The Great Silence which was to be "especially observed."

For me, protection of one's right to solitude, peace and quiet was one of nun-life's finest features. I liked the convent idea of keeping women generally undisturbed by unnecessary and unwanted distractions. As the rule book wisely noted, "Conversational powers are no common gift, especially among women meeting daily in the same circle." The rule book also said those living in the presence of God, would "never disturb anyone unnecessarily and would show love of silence by the noiseless way in which they moved and acted." If it was necessary to speak, nuns were to do so "briefly and in low tones."

In addition to a pretty mean no-talking rule, nun silence also meant generally not disturbing others by calling attention to yourself in any way at all (e.g., loud sneezes, extra loud laughs, hand and eye signals). Nuns were to "conduct themselves with becoming gravity, avoiding in speech and action all frivolity and whatever may attract undo attention." Well, for some that just about covered their whole life. For some, becoming silent called for quite a few profound personal adjustments. You don't really know how much noise your life makes until there's

Examples of individuals who would've been nailed for failure to conduct themselves with BECOMING GRAVITY.

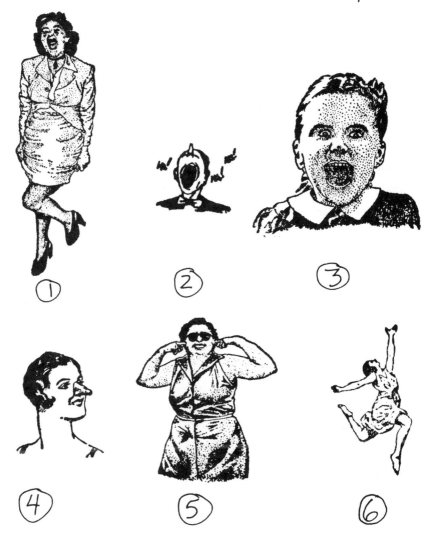

absolute silence—or until Sister called you aside and told you.

By day, then, communal protection of the right to silence often provided a great atmosphere to focus, concentrate and do your work. By night it often provided endless hours of hearing nothing but yourself think. Part of me still believes The Great Silence rule was made up to keep monks and nuns from complaining at the end of the day when many were tired, and some sick and tired.

While many nuns were indeed so tired at the end of the day they could hardly speak, others were so wound up at the end of the day they could hardly sleep. Being wrapped in The Great Silence either knocked you out and left you to rest in peace, or kept you awake because all you could hear was yourself thinking. That's when not being able to talk nearly killed me. That's also when I started writing at the end of every day. As a baby nun it saved me from exploding and going crazy and has continued to serve that function ever since, thus earning a most significant place among the ten best things to do before you die.

What to Write

What to write never presents much of a problem if you can listen to yourself think. That's the trick. And nothing amplifies the opportunity to hear yourself think more than The Great Silence. Try it. When the day is close to over (an hour or two before bedtime), go somewhere greatly silent and re-run the day like a movie in your mind. Then make lists—two of them. While watching the movie with your mind's eye, make a list of the best parts of the day and the worst parts of the day. Then, remembering what you did with both, elaborate.

Now when it comes to describing what you loved most about the best parts and hated most about the worst parts, don't hesitate to write your bloody little heart out. Also include any other strange and interesting parts of the day worth remembering. All in all that's a good solid night's work. A minimum of one hour is a good lifetime goal, one half hour or less in circumstances where Great Silence is virtually impossible.

Why Every Day?

Connected to the nun habit of The Great Silence is the monthly and annual nun habit of retreat. One day each month and an extended time annually is set aside for retreat. Interspersed through the year are additional special days of *solemn* retreat, my favorite one being New Year's Eve.

The difference between retreat days and regular nun days was one of my first questions as a new nun. It turned out retreat days were like days off from work, which meant that except for a few communal prayer and meal events, the day was pretty much your own. Free free free days. Big chunks of unscheduled time. And New Year's Eve was one of the least scheduled solemn retreat days of all, thus heading the top of my Favorite Retreat Days list. Solemnly retreating was also a purely contrary and outrageous thing to do on New Year's Eve, further enhancing its significance.

Now the very best part of retreat days was the free time. Huge chunks of time provided hour upon solitary hour for reading through all the lists of bests and worsts and conducting "The Best and Worst of the Month Review." Then, on New Year's Eve, "The Annual Best and Worst of the Year Awards." What a

49

gala event that is. Both are tremendously insightful and entertaining exercises because there are few things more stunning and funny than seeing yourself and others in perspective.

Of course the more faithful you are to the daily exercise, Sister said, the more insightful and enjoyable the reviews, which is why one must strive to write at the end of every day. Plus, writing at the end of every day is the only way the habit of doing so can be acquired. And nun or not, this is one habit well worth acquiring before you die.

EVERY WORD BORN
OF AN INNER NECESSITY—

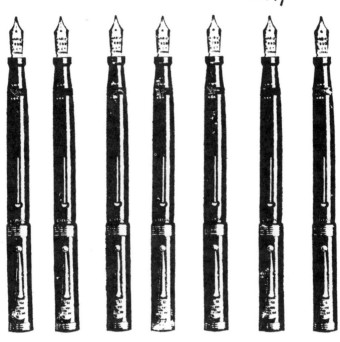

WRITING MUST never Be anything else.

etty HILLESUM
an interrupted life

Sixth Thing:

Think About Being a Nun*

You think about being a nun far more after entering the convent than before. Then you've really got something to think about. At 18, all I knew about being a nun was that it mostly meant none of this and none of that and I got picked to be one. I also noticed some nuns in high school who were very smart, very well traveled, did very good work (and late at night), and most importantly looked like they were having a lot of fun.

Other than that, nun life was one big mysterious well-guarded secret. Even once I was in the convent it

---

*Even though boys can't be nuns, that does not excuse the male reader from thinking about it before he dies. The three good reasons for being a nun are pretty androgynous, and more than anything else seek to cultivate and strengthen the feminine aspects of the psyche, regardless of gender.

was only revealed bit by bit. Good thing. If everything was revealed all at once, it would have been way too much—probably nobody would've joined. Most likely we would never do anything if we knew ahead of time all we'd have to go through. Lots of people stop dead short and settle for less: Take whatever you can while you can because nothing is meant to last forever.

Well, I never believed that and neither did nuns. Nuns don't believe a lot of things the rest of the world believes. That weird mysterious other-world dimension of nun life held the greatest attraction for me—communities of strange, plain-looking women living together on the fringe of society, doing very brave and interesting work, all the time giving strong evidence of having discovered some deep dark secret to life which had a lot to do with God, and a God that seemed fun to be with. In 1964 that looked like the thing for me to do so I joined those sisters (of the Holy Cross), and still do join them.

People think the most interesting question you can ask a nun is, "Why did you enter the convent?" Wrong. Ask why they stay. That's much harder and far more interesting. If you promise to do something forever and lose sight of the only reason for doing it, you seriously risk missing the whole point and getting lost in looking and feeling like a nun but behaving any old way you want—a deadly disease in every way of life and not at all a hard one to catch. Once upon a time, in referring to herself, her chubby nun friends, and the thought of changing the habit, a dear dearer dearest old nun confided, "Oh, but Sister, the habit covers a multitude of sins." I never forgot that.

All the good reasons I know to keep being a nun have to do with three big things nuns believe that the rest of the world mostly doesn't. Even if there's absolutely no chance you'll be a nun, these are well worth thinking about anyhow because oftentimes what you don't know will eventually hurt you—and everyone else connected to you.

Three Good Reasons to Be a Nun

1. *All Nuns Are Treated Equal*

Nuns do not believe the one who dies with the most things wins. Nuns also don't care about cutest, tannest, thinnest, most fashionable, most money, most anything. For nuns, with the exception of your very best self, your very best God and your very best work, *mores* and *mosts* and *bests* hardly ever mean better, and the vow of poverty ensures that that will always and forever be the case. The non-competitive, evenly equal nature of nun life is clearly one of its finest features, particularly for women, who have to spend tons of time and energy everywhere else competing and struggling for equality.

A big part of being treated equal has to do with the nun belief that what binds people together is infinitely more important than what sets them apart. Nuns, and others like them in this regard, treasure commonalities more than differences, which is both a blessing and a curse. The trick is to let the commonalities bind us peacefully together while letting the differences delight us, enrich us, educate us and keep us alive.

Binding and loosing—controlling the flock by putting them in a large pasture—that's the real trick. It's also one of those areas where what you find outside the convent, you'll pretty much find inside the convent, only slightly better controlled and far more subtle. Binding is usually believed to be safely known and obviously good, whereas loosing is usually believed to be frighteningly unknown and subtly evil. Nuns believe the twain between the two meets in carefully giving each what she needs even though each need is different. That's real true equality. Treating all nuns equal is so important it was made into a vow and called poverty.

One practical bonus to being treated equal is the relative freedom from anxiety about money. That can never be underestimated. There are nuns (God bless and keep them) whose job it is to worry about money which directly relieves that burden from the rest of us. Then, regardless of how much nuns earn, it all goes into a common fund from which each sister gets what she asks for: sometimes more, sometimes less. Having too much is always discouraged, mostly to prevent the consumption of clever nuns by *more more more*. It's also pretty confusing to see nuns with more and better things than anyone else.

So you see, the pure joy of being treated equal lies in how good it is when everyone has what they need with still some left over for giving away. That's the best and most socially responsible consequence of vowing poverty. And nun or not, I highly recommend vowing some kind of poverty, especially if you have what you need with some left over. Jesus says either give away what you don't really truly need or start trying to stuff yourself through the eye of a needle (Lk 18:25). Take your pick.

2.   *Nuns Aren't Interested in Being Married*

The idea of belonging to another person now or forever never appealed to me, though the basic idea of belonging always has. Being owned was something

CONTINUAL ATTENTION SHALL BE PAID TO

UNIFORMITY,

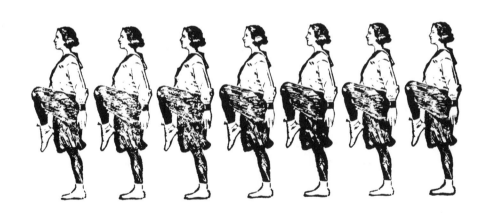

THE NATURAL GUARDIAN OF ORDER AND UNION.

- OLD NUN RULE BOOK -

I never wanted to be and one of the best ways to prevent being owned is to remain unwed. Even the most primitive concepts of liberty involve the right of doing what you want with your life until you marry. Well, I want to be able to do what I want with my life period. No untils. Interestingly enough, the word "virgin" also means an unmarried woman: she who will not have or be had by a husband. Joining ages and ages of holy and not so holy women committed to preserving the divine freedom of the unwed—for me that's a great and brave reason to be a nun.*

With the vow of celibacy nuns go even further on the ownership issue to say you will not be owned by man *or anyone else*, which is why nuns historically go gaga over friendships that "particularly" exclude, isolate, encourage inordinate dependency and consume enormous amounts of time and energy. To believe celibacy is simply a no-marriage, no-sex rule is to miss the whole point. Never merely a physiological or external fact, Sister said, celibacy means no possessiveness, inordinate dependency or exclusiveness at all between you and man and anyone else.

So, while poverty teaches nuns how to treat one another, celibacy teaches nuns how to love one another. And when it comes to loving, nuns firmly believe that excluding, possessing, owning, heavily depending upon, isolating and consuming enormous amounts of time and energy are never good

------

*Plus in 1964, being a nun looked like tons more fun than the other Catholic alternative for unwed women (not men) called "single blessedness," which appeared to be exceedingly boring and lonely.

ways—not in the convent or anywhere else. One who bears divinity in her own right does not need the security of others. That's the nun belief about chastity of soul and the main reason nuns don't marry.

Now, when it comes to women and their ways of loving, nuns are pretty much like women everywhere, only once again generally more controlled, more subtle and, because of the intensity of the religious element, probably far more complex. According to the nun belief about chastity of soul, any woman who lives her life in order to please others, be accepted, gain power, be liked, and win another's interest and love is no virgin. You can now see why getting insight and getting depth are especially critical developmental tasks for nuns. There's no being a virgin without them.

If you still wonder why anyone would ever want to be celibate, the two best answers can be found in looking at Mary, Mother of God and Virgin extraordinaire. There are two incredibly attractive things about Mary, which older Catholics learned early on. First, there's something magical and mysterious about Mary's virginity, because ordinary sexual experiences (marriage and childbearing) do not touch her, do not make her any less a virgin. In some mysterious and unexplained fashion, the mother of Jesus and wife of Joseph remains forever virgin.

Second, Mary is so compassionate that she hides repentant sinners in her full skirt, thus sneaking them into heaven past the righteous hand of God. Mary's virginity is so powerful it becomes the undoing of God himself. That's why Catholics prayed to Mary constantly. And why little Catholic girls couldn't wait to join the Children of Mary. When you can't get something from God, always turn to the Mother of

God—even if you run out of wine at a party (Jn 2:10).

So, while celibacy may look like nothing from nothing leaves nothing, *nothing* could be farther from the truth. For those who retain virginity as Mary did, an exceedingly difficult, divine and glorious life is promised, full of mysterious and incredible events, not the least of which is compassion, the profoundly intimate and tender undoing of God himself.

The mysteriousness of virginity has a lot to do with implicit trust of life events as somehow divine, even when they bring confusion, misery, pain and death. Like the Virgin Mary, nuns (particularly Sisters of the Holy Cross) believe that the energies which shatter life are just as precious and divine as those which gather life together again. The dark face of God is just as lovely as the radiant shining face of God. Darkness and light are incredibly the same, both essential to the perpetual renewal of life: sorrows into joys . . . endings into beginnings . . . winters into springs . . . ups into downs . . . nights into days . . . food into fat. There clearly is a purpose for everything under heaven.

So, like Mary, Mother of God and Virgin extraordinaire, nuns believe compassion is the very best way to cope with all of life's ups, downs and uncertainties. It's what real true celibacy looks like. Jesus says compassion is also what God looks like (Lk 6:36), the closest we can get to being divine. Being able to accept reverently, creatively and sympathetically all of life's passions and pains made the Virgin Mary so divine she ended up indestructible. Death could not touch her. Unable to die, the Catholic church says she was assumed into heaven. Or just assumed she went to heaven—whatever.

TOWARDS THE MOON IT IS
   YOU SHOULD LOOK,
YOU WHO ARE BURIED IN THE SHADOW
   OF SIN AND INIQUITY.
HAVING LOST DIVINE GRACE,
   THE DAY DISAPPEARS,
THERE IS NO MORE SUN FOR YOU;
   BUT THE MOON IS STILL IN THE HORIZON.
      ADDRESS YOURSELF
        TO MARY;
     UNDER HER INFLUENCE
THOUSANDS EVERY DAY
      FIND THEIR WAY
      TO GOD.

 POPE INNOCENT III

Well, there you have it. Nuns aren't interested in being married, because celibacy preserves the divine freedom of the unwed, fills life with mysterious and incredible events, generates infinitely compassionate lives and works, assumes women into heaven while still on earth, and last but not least, saves women from the devastating and deadly effects of having and being had. Now you tell me, what woman in her right mind wouldn't want that?

3. *Nuns Listen to God*
    More Than to Anyone Else

The third good reason to be a nun has to do with obedience and how nuns believe it's exceedingly important to listen to God more than to anyone else. "Which God?" is always the big question. Up until recently, well established voices of authority (church, government, family) were believed to be pretty representative of the voice of God on earth. Consequently, blind unquestioning obedience to those "legitimate" voices was proclaimed the greatest of virtues. Question everything but authority. We can see now those were not the good old days.

Now, the traditionally sacred institutions of legitimate truth are in crisis. The "infallible" voices of authority in every major sector of American life have fallen from grace: TV's evangelical pillars of faith; dissenting nuns, priests, bishops, cardinals and archbishops; the federal government's Iran-Contra deal and God knows what other deals; and the marked increase in troubled, abusive, dysfunctional families.

In each case, unquestioning obedience to the voice of religious, civic and parental authority has lost its credibility almost completely, leaving millions of

SIGN ON CONVENT DOOR.

ILLUSTRATED BY FAIRYGODCHILD ELLEN SEREMET
AGE 6

hopelessly devoted followers confused, forsaken, angry and alone. Yet, when authoritative voices dissent or are proven fallible, the importance of one's own inner voice becomes critical and equally troublesome. When the voice of authority demands something quite different from the inner voice, the voice of God, with which do we comply?

Nuns have worked out an exceptionally good answer to that question and it's no longer simply, "Whatever Sister says." No matter the question, nuns now and always firmly believe in listening to God more than to anyone else. "How do you know you're listening to God and not yourself?" That's the next most frequently asked question. The nun answer to that question however remains the same: "Whatever Sister says." Listening to God more than anyone else is what nuns call discernment and when nuns discern alone and together over the same issue, it usually becomes pretty clear what's really God and what's merely self-interest in disguise.

Weighing pros and cons alone and together is a mysterious, incredibly reliable way to figure out God's will. Discerning obedience helps you to see what you don't want to see, to understand perspectives much different than your own. It also prevents every nun from making God in her own image and likeness. Mostly it just saves you from plain old ordinary stupidity. By virtue of listening to God and one another, the compassionate bonds of sisterhood are loosened, preserved and strengthened.

A Word About Holy Disobedience [1]

The hardest part of listening to God more than to anyone else comes when the voice of God does indeed demand something different from the voice of authority. How regrettable not to have a comparable theology of disobedience to help discern and understand non-compliance with authority as God's will. The Old Testament instinct to strike dead all who challenge authority still haunts us and fear of widespread insubordination continues to determine public policy and practice. Those elements of the patriarchy remain profoundly entrenched.

For true nuns, however, the answer to the God vs. authority standoff remains the same. Obedience. Nuns listen to God more than anyone else. Like Mary, ever the faithful virgin, the bottom line is this: No one but God tells nuns or other virgins what to do. In that regard, nuns continue the old biblical tradition of women liberators like Esther and Judith, for whom deception and disobedience work as the will of God. When nuns find the demands of "authority" in conflict with what they know to be the will of God, individual and communal discernment gets pretty intense.

Discerning why one chooses to disobey the voice of authority (or the voice of God) is by far the most interesting, mysterious and compelling aspect of obedience. In the Book of Esther, four pretty clear reasons appear which prompt holy disobedience: The situation is unbearable and survival is at stake; the voice of God promises deliverance; the contemplated act of disobedience would relieve oppression; and last but certainly not least, divine intervention is not at all likely.

From biblical liberators like Esther and Judith, we learn that the soul of the obedient one lies in solidarity with the oppressed, because that's where God's voice cries out loud and clear: "You are the God of the humble, the help of the oppressed, the support of the weak, the refuge of the forsaken, the Savior of the despairing" (Jdt 9:11). For all liberators, past and present, the only legitimate reasons for disobedience, trickery and deception are religious ones, those that come from God and contain the moral imperative to set the oppressed free.

So for nuns, holy obedience and holy disobedience are really one and the same. The only thing that ever matters is listening to God more than to anyone else. And, given the shape of authority in this world, that's not a bad thing for everyone to think about doing before and until they die. If everyone in the world listened to God more than to anyone else, what an event that would be. The whole world could be assumed into heaven. Or you could just assume that would be heaven. Whatever.

Now What Do You Think About Being a Nun?

So there you have it: three perfectly good reasons to be a nun. Even if you still don't want to be one, you must admit that the nun life is far more interesting to think about than it's given credit for. And those are just three of the reasons. There are others. In addition to the "gifts" of poverty, celibacy and obedience, there's also a wealth of moral support, everlasting friendship and corporate solidarity, all of which are extremely difficult to find if you try to live the nun life alone.

On August 15, 1972, feast of the Assumption of Mary and former final profession day for Sisters of the Holy Cross, there was a part in the vow ceremony where the bishop, reading from the gospel of John, told us that if we kept the promises just made ". . . there would be gifts for us. Gifts that no one can take

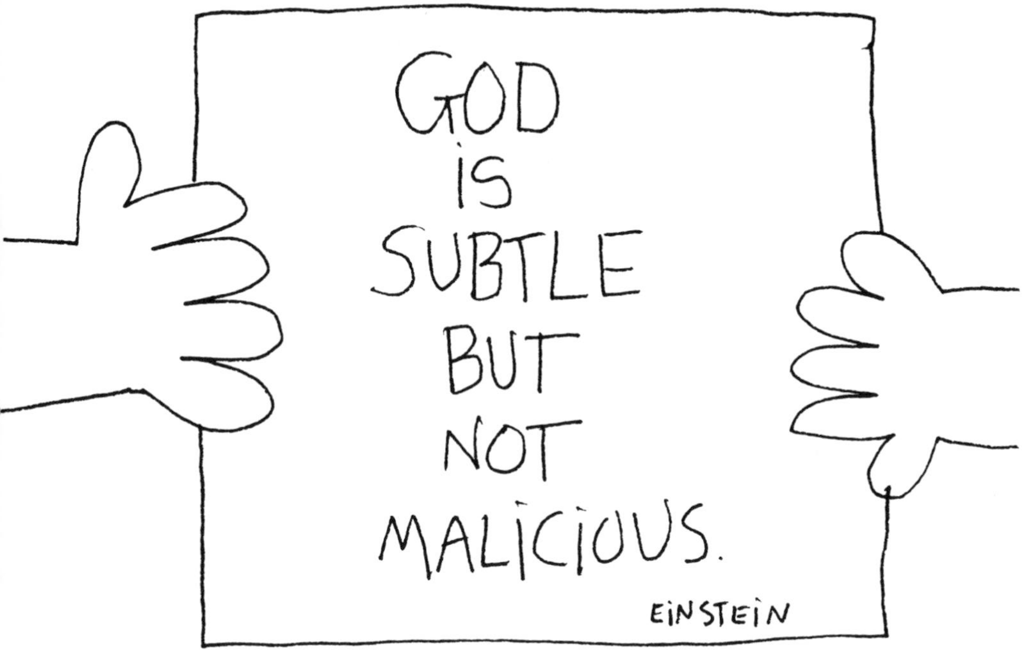
GOD
IS
SUBTLE
BUT
NOT
MALICIOUS.
EINSTEIN

away." At the time a few of us thought no one could take them away because no one in their right mind—except us—would want them. We signed a paper stating we were in our right minds and still wanted them. Kind of like climbing to the top of the highest mountain and throwing yourself into the abyss. Freaking crazy.

The bishop then confirmed that we were indeed fools, but reminded us that ". . . the things of God always look foolish and crazy to human beings. The message of the cross is complete absurdity to those headed for ruin, but to us (Sisters of the Holy Cross), it is the power of God" (cf. 1 Cor 1:18, 25).

Well, that was nowhere near the comfort then that it is now. Maybe it just takes almost 25 years to understand what real true foolishness is. Whatever. If well lived, the nun life is clearly more wonderful than all that can be said of it, and really deserves to be thought about before you die. Especially if all you think it means is none of this and none of that and you'll never get picked to be one.

---

[1]The idea for this section comes from my article, "Holy Disobedience in the Book of Esther," in *Theology Today*, Princeton, N.J., January, 1989.

Seventh Thing:

Make Yourself Interesting

Making yourself interesting, as you probably do not recall, is one of the two main ingredients to being a fun person. This is one of the four main ingredients to having more fun than anyone else, which is number one on this list of Ten Things to Do Before You Die. Make yourself interesting.

Sometimes I think the most tragic human flaw lies in the slothful belief that some people automatically grow up interesting and others don't. Wrong wrong wrong. No one automatically grows up anything except boring, which is frightfully like the salt of the earth going flat. How can you restore its flavor? You can't. "It is good for nothing, and can only be thrown out to be trampled underfoot" (Mt 5:13), a clear indication of the terminally deadening effects of boredom.

While hard work at first, making yourself interesting is exceedingly important to do before you die because it prevents your going flat, becoming good for nothing, being thrown out and trampled underfoot—never a very pretty picture. With an infinite number of ways to make yourself interesting, it once again took 42 years to find four:

1. *Cultivate a Diverse Group of Friends*

What better way to make yourself interesting and further the cause of true equality than to cultivate a diverse group of friends. While commonalities do indeed bind people peacefully together, remember, the differences delight us, enrich us, educate us, and keep us alive. Associating only with your own kind breeds many unattractive and narrow features, not the least of which is boring boring boring: All the same with no distinguishing features. This invokes the wrath of God because the same is absolutely not how God creates. Like the person with no insight, the boring "lukewarm" individual also makes God mad enough to spit them out (Rv 3:16-17).

Nuns tend to be extra good at cultivating diverse groups of friends because, God knows, if there's anyone who lives with real diverse types, it's nuns. Think of all the nuns you know. Most likely some other nuns live with them. So nuns learn right away how to accept and live with all kinds. That's one of the main jobs of a nun: Treat everyone like an angel of God, like Jesus Christ—the rich, the poor, "the tired, huddled masses yearning to breathe free," the lost and the found, "the wretched refuse of your teeming shores," sinner and tax collector, even "the tempest tossed."

With regard to all, every sister should be a Sister of Mercy. No sister should do to others what she would not like to have done to herself, and, on the same principle, every sister should do to others precisely what she would wish to have done to herself.

70

A
JOYFUL
(i.e. fun)
 HEART
IS THE HEALTH
OF THE BODY,
BUT A DEPRESSED
(i.e. BORING)
SPIRIT
DRIES UP THE BONES.

(YOUR OWN AND EVERYBODY ELSE'S).

PROVERBS 17:22

That's the attitude necessary to cultivate a truly diverse and interesting group of friends.

Now take a quick look at your circle of friends. If all tend to be like you (e.g., cheerleaders, pompom girls, prom queens), or if you don't have any friends at all, you could be well on your way to developing a cute but noticeably boring life. If your friends are quite different than you (e.g., bagpipe player, nun, athlete), chances are your life will be increasingly jampacked and fun filled. So work hard on cultivating a diverse group of friends. You're likely to end up like salt gone flat if you don't, good for nothing but to be thrown out and trampled underfoot. One clear tragic waste of humanity.

2. *Work*

Finding your very best work is the third of the three biggest bests to find, the other two being your very best self and God. All three go together and cannot survive one apart from the other. Much more than earning a living, work means using your body or mind (preferably both) to accomplish some life task. Work is what you do with your life and not what life does with you.

With regard to making yourself interesting, work is an essential ingredient. If your work is interesting and those you work with fun, it will contribute immeasurably to your becoming an interesting and fun person. Unusual and unpredictable things tend to happen with fun interesting people, making for enjoyment now and great storytelling later. Great storytelling, as you also probably do not recall, is one of the hallmarks of a fun person.

If, on the other hand, you find work and those you work with pretty lifeless and boring, that also will

SAD BUT TRUE

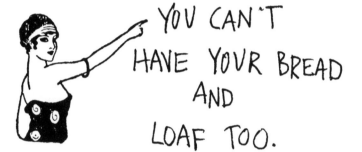

YOU CAN'T
HAVE YOUR BREAD
AND
LOAF TOO.

GOD

contribute immeasurably to you yourself becoming a pretty lifeless and boring person. When work is indeed a real snore and not much ever happens that's worth retelling later, you are likely to be lulled to sleep, drawn day by day into the deadly den of boredom. If the rest of life is also a real snore with not much ever happening that's worth retelling, there's precious little hope for restoring life's flavor, sad to say.

The only thing worse than a boring work plus a boring life is a boring life plus no work at all, the ultimate in nothing. With no activity at all to engage body and mind, one can slip rather quickly and unconsciously into an increasingly vegetative, decadent state. Without any kind of work whatsoever most are consumed by the incredibly strong tendency to loaf, vegetate, watch T.V., eat snacks, shop and take naps—or do sex, drugs, rock and roll. Decadence, utter decadence.

While sometimes recommendable in small doses, decadence does nothing more than slowly kill you with its well-disguised, consuming boredom. In much the same way, the excessive worker is slowly killed by not-so-well-disguised exhaustion, a whole other kind of boredom. The trick is to find your very best work (e.g., parenting, teaching, healing, writing, plumbing) and consistently give it your very best self. What you end up with then is your very best creative work ever, which is always of infinite interest.

3. *Educate Yourself*

The worst thing you can ever do to yourself is feel completely educated after grade school, high school, years of college or degree of degrees. The very minute you stop learning is the very minute you start becoming ignorant again. Boring boring boring.

74

Regardless of seemingly endless years of schooling, we absolutely must continue to educate ourselves if we ever expect to be interesting persons capable of having more fun than anyone else.

Right off the bat I can think of five ways to continue to learn, that with some effort and a little bit of money could easily fit into an ordinary day or life.

1. Read at least an hour every day
2. See lots of movies
3. Do theatre, galleries, museums and concerts
4. Take classes
5. Travel

Then there's always learning from experience, especially mistakes. That kind of learning can be accomplished for free and at any time at all. Forever continuing your education is such an absolute must because it helps keep mind, body and soul alive. Without it you have increasingly less to say and could easily end up grunting and groaning your way into old age. Not at all a very pretty or pleasant way to go.

4. *Take Sides*

In accepting the Nobel Peace Prize on December 10, 1986, Holocaust survivor Elie Wiesel made the *New York Times* "Quotation of the Day" with these words:

Take sides.
Neutrality helps the oppressor,
never the victim.
Silence encourages the tormentor,
never the tormented.

The Holocaust is one colossal tragically clear consequence of humanity's failure to take sides . . . all of humanity without exception. Makes you wonder

75

if silence and neutrality are ever the virtues they appear to be. Makes you wonder if maybe they're just a polite, saintly looking way of avoiding conflict, fearing the consequences of truth, finding possible rejection unbearable—or simply protecting yourself from God only knows what.

We can see now that the consequences of "keeping the peace" and avoiding conflict are destructive and deadly beyond our wildest imaginings. Clearly and with great urgency, taking sides is the virtue to be cultivated now and for the future. Remember, the "lukewarm," those who are "neither hot nor cold," get spewed from the mouth of God. They simply make God sick.

One important thing to keep in mind when taking sides is to pick battles carefully. Taking sides on every little thing that passes by means you're not very likely to get much work done and will probably be crazy in 48 hours or less. Taking sides all day long misses the point. Just take sides on important stuff, stuff that touches your very best self, very best God and very strongest convictions. The time for silence, neutrality and peace of mind comes only after doing all you can. The rest is not up to you. Then comes the time for keeping still, going with the flow, learning patience and perseverance day by day by day.

The most interesting, enjoyable and admirable people are those brave enough to take sides. The most boring, infuriating and deceptive people are those who believe their messianic role in life is to keep the peace. Make nice. Maintain neutrality. Win popularity contests. Get crowned Miss Congeniality. Never ever ever take sides.

That passively passive posture is nearly always

disturbing and deadening, hardly ever peacekeeping or peacemaking, and never interesting or fun. God says if we're not for him, then we are clearly against him. And those who refuse to take sides are doomed to the ranks of the neutral lukewarms who get spewed out in the end. Ptooey. Ptooey. Ptooey.

Hopefully you can see now that making yourself interesting takes considerable thought and effort and is exceedingly important to do before you die. Unless, that is, you want to go flat, lose your flavor, and be good for nothing but to be thrown out and trampled underfoot. Either that or be spewed from the mouth of God. Both are good as dead.

The choice set before Israel is also ours: "Here then I have set before you," says God, "life and prosperity, death and doom. . . If you listen to your God you will live [a very interesting life]. If, however, you turn away your hearts and will not listen, you will certainly perish [from boredom, for starters]. I have set before you life and death, the blessing and the curse" (cf. Dt 30:15-20 NAB). God then, of course, recommends always choosing life so that we may live an exceedingly interesting life and never fall under the boring spell of "the curse." To listen to our very best self and God or not, that's the everlasting choice which always makes us and life very interesting.

BECAUSE YOU ARE LUKEWARM,
NEITHER HOT NOR COLD,
I WILL SPEW YOU OUT OF
MY MOUTH....

REVELATION
3:16

Eighth Thing:

Live Alone for a While

Because it's a rare person who wants to live alone now or forever, living alone for a while is a profoundly important thing to do regularly before you die. And living alone forever is certainly worth some serious thought—especially by women for whom regular periods of solitude are a psychological necessity, an inborn need.

For as far back as history goes, there's nearly always been some kind of seclusion prescribed for women, usually in the form of menstrual taboos. Women were so powerfully scary then, men couldn't stand it. Sending the women way off to these hermitage-like huts one week a month was the answer. Get rid of what scares and undoes you. Make it taboo.

What a deal for the woman, however. That's three months' vacation. Plus, all those scary menstrual women living together every month for a week in the same area, fasting, doing other purification rites, and only God knows what else—now there's an interesting idea! Primitive women's clubs. Maybe early primitive convents. Quite possibly the divine origins of the nun's monthly time for retreat over and above the regular silent nun days.

Some people believe women themselves initiated the taboo by making men crazy on purpose. Acting really weird would justify getting away from it all for a while. Another great idea. Whatever the reason, the main point is that women clearly and regularly need to isolate themselves from the insistent demands of family, friends and work. Preserving and nurturing the feminine value for solitude, for a "room of one's own," is essential now and has been for as long as we know. Living alone is clearly no new concept in women's lives.

The Best Parts of Living Alone

The very best part of living alone lies in its provision of endless solitude. What does solitude mean for the tabooed woman and what does the tabooed woman's solitude mean for the life of family, friends and work?

1. *Finding Peace and Quiet*

The peace and quiet dimension of living alone is clearly one of its finest features, often having a calming, comforting, liberating effect. By allowing one to withdraw physically and emotionally from the constant personal demands of family, friends and co-workers, solitude offers instant comfort and rest for the soul. The demanding voices of others are silenced and only the "still, small voice" of your very best self and God remains. The "still, small" sound of that voice is oftentimes so soothing that to withdraw in this way clearly produces a strangely calming, restful, healing effect—a bit of eternal rest.

But even if you don't withdraw in this way, there's still the pure simple fact of peace and quiet with all its ordinary well-being, and that can certainly be enough. Peace and quiet saves women from losing themselves in the needs and demands of others and also prevents life from becoming nothing more than the oppressive sum of its way-too-many parts. Peace and quiet is indeed its own reward.

2. *Finding God*

In the Bible, the call to solitude is always an invitation to get in touch with your very best self and God. The Lord tells the prophet Hosea, "I am going to seduce her and lead her into the desert and speak to her heart" (Hos 2:16). The God of Isaiah pleads, "Go into your private room, shut yourselves in. Hide yourselves a little while" (Is 26:20). Jesus encouraged the disciples to "Come away to some lonely place all by yourselves and rest for a while" (Mk 6:31). "Go to your private room, shut yourselves in, and so pray to God . . . who is in that secret place" (Mt 6:6).

When we're alone and isolated from all life's demands and disturbances, clearly God guides us to solitude, and solitude can gradually lead us to God. "I did not find You without, Lord," St. Augustine prayed, "because I wrongly sought You without, who were within." Living alone can offer undivided and unlimited access to God abiding within. Probably the scariest and most comforting of the best parts of living alone.

81

JMJ

ON LIVING ALONE

BY JOHN OF THE CROSS

She lived in solitude,
And now in solitude has
    Built her nest;
And in solitude God guides her,
 God alone, who also bears
In solitude, the wound of love.

3. *Finding Yourself*

That little piece "On Living Alone" is the saint's gentle poetic way of informing us that while solitude can indeed produce a strangely peaceful, calming, loving effect, it can also never fail to confront us with a whole host of ghosts: fears, adversaries, troubles and wounds; our own truth, depth and limits; the internal barriers (attitudes, needs, dependencies) which keep us from our very best self and God.

One of the less attractive and less courageous features of the human spirit is its tendency to forever blame misery on someone else—men or women in general; husbands, wives, children and friends in particular. By virtue of living alone, however, there is no one else upon which to inflict your misery. Just you yourself, your very best God, and possibly a pet. Therein lies the best and worst part of living alone. The good divine you living side by side with all the mistakes of your own making. Absolutely nothing can reveal those dark and light truths quite like the solitude that comes with living alone.

Now if you refuse to pay attention to solitude's revelations and confrontations, slowly but surely you will be driven crazy, to the point where you become unlivable to everyone including yourself. Because the "still, small voice" of your best self and God cannot be silenced, to listen or not to listen is probably the most decisive experience of all.

The very best advice now and forever is to save yourself a lot of time and trouble and pay attention to whatever solitude puts before you. Meeting the biggest fears, adversaries, troubles and wounds is far less disturbing than never knowing for sure what they are, where they come from or why they're there. Plus, like the dirt that comes with the digging, the disturbances all become exceedingly precious after awhile, gradually making the solitary one stronger, braver, freer, more indestructible. Remember: The only thing we have to fear is fat itself. And that's the truth.

4.   *Finding New Energy*

In the end, the solitary one finds new energy in solitude, and that very same new energy is what solitude means for the life of family, friends and work. With the finding of peace, quiet, God and self, one also gradually discovers the pure ecstasy of being able to accept what is, to trust the life force even when it sounds its worst misery. Just go go go with the flow flow flow.

Sometimes new ways to resolve life's difficulties are found in solitude. Other times you may find there's no advantage in doing anything; it's best to just keep still. "I charge you, daughters of Jerusalem, do not rouse, do not wake my beloved, before she pleases!" (Sg 8:4). The outcome in any case is that divine energy becomes available for life. New energy flows into relationships, deepening and strengthening them, oftentimes overflowing into all kinds of creative work.

The solitary one who retreats beleaguered, worn out and drained comes out feeling pretty mysteriously brand new. In the "Song of Songs," the woman coming out of solitude is hardly even recognizable to her maiden friends who ask, "Who is this coming up from the desert, leaning on her lover?" (Sg 8:5).

"Grace" is what the new single-hearted energy looks like. "Tranquil beauty" according to the *I Ching*—clarity within, quiet without;[1] the gift of God which contains all other gifts. "Your faithful love is better than life itself" (Ps 63:3). Simple amazing grace.

THE FINAL WORD

I think that I'll do it anyway:

I'll turn inwards for half an hour...
and listen to my inner voice.
   Lose myself. You could also call
   it meditation. I am still a bit wary
of that word. But anyway, why not?
A quiet half-hour within yourself.
   It's not enough to move your

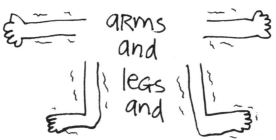

arms
and
legs
and

all other muscles.... we are body
and spirit... what really matters
is our soul or essence or
whatever else you care to call
what shines through from within.

etty hillesum
an interrupted life

Better than life itself. Fuller and richer than all our experiences put together. And, regardless of how grace feels or doesn't feel, God assured St. Paul, "My grace is enough for you, for my power is at full strength in weakness" (2 Cor 12:9). So whatever the solitary one brings back to the life of family, friends and work, it all somehow ends up being compassionately and mercifully enough. Sometimes more than enough. Sometimes seemingly never enough. But always and forever mysteriously enough. "God is perfectly able to enrich you with every grace, so that you always have enough for every conceivable need, and your surplus overflow in all kinds of good work" (2 Cor 9:8). One of the very best parts of living alone now and forever clearly lies in how true solitude welcomes you home, gives you rest, then lifts you up, carries you through and returns you back to ordinary life pretty brand new. That's my idea of a real good time.

The Worst Parts of Living Alone

Well, as life would have it, for every set of bests, there's likely to be a comparable set of worsts. Strengths and weaknesses, bests and worsts—clearly just two faces of the same moon, two sides of the same coin, two parts of the same day. While the list of bests demonstrates the glorious parts of living alone, the list of worsts demonstrates the not-so-glorious, sometimes awful parts of living alone. I know four of those also:

1. *It's Hard Work*

Because there's no one else home to lend a hand with the things you hate doing, living alone means you do *all* housework yourself: pay bills, keep the accounts, take care of the car, clean house (windows, walls, floors), do laundry, shop, cook, do dishes, learn to fix things, take care of the dog, shovel snow, rake leaves, mow the lawn, answer the phone and door, kill the bats, set and dispose of mouse traps. Not to mention unexpected crises, like a Wednesday night at 9:24 when the living room ceiling falls on the living room floor.

In any event, it's just you you you and possibly a pet (who, when it comes to housework is good for absolutely nothing). Living in a group usually means only having to do a few of those things and pretty much being able to pick the jobs you like. Living alone is full of sometimes very hard and always very bothersome, time-consuming work. Housework is clearly the solitary one's worst enemy.

2. *It's More Stressful*

Practically everything written on stress these days tells how the load is greatest among those who live alone. No big surprise there. When it's just you with no one else around it takes real effort to focus on something other than how you feel or what happened that day. Happy or sad, when all you hear is yourself thinking, too much of that good thing can make you crazy. It can push you to the limit where enough is enough is enough. That's when you flip back to the fourth thing to do before you die, find a place to escape reality, and don't come back until you have to.

Finding ways to cope all alone in your tiny tiny house is one of life's greatest and most profound challenges. Eating and drinking are scary ways of coping, especially if you remember the only thing we have to fear is fat itself. The wonderful and nearly extinct world of the foaming bath or hot tub is a glorious escape well worth immediate discovery, as are all kinds of music, reading, cooking, writing, movies, plays and sacred games (*I Ching*, The Tarot, Runes). All are surprisingly delightful ways to enjoy continually the pleasure of your own company.

3. *It's Sometimes Lonely*

Living alone is sometimes lonely, sometimes terribly lonely. But then again, living in a group is also sometimes lonely, and sometimes terribly lonely. Alone or not, loneliness is a fact of life that goes as far back as the Garden of Eden, which is practically as far back as the mind can go. Being alone is another one of those gifts no one can take away because who wants it? Learning to live with loneliness never ever quite takes it completely away, just makes it less mean and far less pathetic.

In all kinds of ways, "it is not right that one should be alone" (Gn 2:18). Clearly, parts of living alone lend themselves to isolation, self-indulgence and a certain carelessness about life. If it doesn't bother me, why should it bother anyone else? Living alone is a perfect setup for massive escape, but hardly ever ends up that way for long because it's mostly yourself you destroy in the end.

The loneliest parts of solitude are clearly those which call for absolute confidence in God (Est 4:16), who abandons the sinner to solitude (Hos 2:5), then does not rest until the lost solitary sheep is found (Lk 15:4). Being lonely is the dark side of being together just as being lost is the dark side of being found. All are part of the movement of life, but nonetheless the hardest and worst parts of living alone.

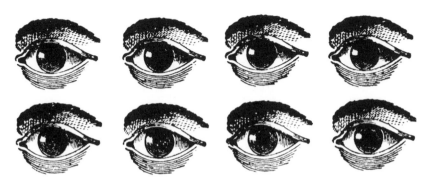

GOD WILL COME
WHEN HE IS NO
LONGER NECESSARY.

KAFKA

4. It's More Expensive

The fact that it costs more to live alone is not fair and often becomes its most discouraging feature. Because no one throws "showers" for people who live alone, you need to buy towels, sheets, blankets, tablecloths, napkins, baking pans, mixing bowls, glasses, dishes, silverware, pots and pans, all major and minor appliances, place mats, hundreds of dollars in kitchen utensils and everything else needed to make a house work. That's expensive.

Plus *all* the house jobs that need to be done gradually are so out-of-control big that it becomes necessary to pay people to help clean house, rake leaves, shovel snow, do laundry, paint, fix and install things. The cost of living a simple life alone is more expensive than living in a group even though you often end up living far more simply when alone. For one who lives alone, that just never seems fair. It's so unfair it makes you wonder about a worldwide conspiracy against solitude in any way, shape or form. The economic sanction for solitude is often a most effective one, especially for nuns and others with simple lifestyles and limited resources. More expensive is absolutely one of the worst and most unfair parts of living alone.

The Bottom Line

Well, now you can see that living alone is and isn't all it's cracked up to be. While finding peace and quiet, God, self and new energy, the solitary one also finds more work, more stress, sometimes more loneliness and always more expense. Damned if you do and damned if you don't. But when it comes to living alone for a while, it is far better to be damned if you do than damned if you don't—so much better that living alone for a while should be required of every adult, a rite of initiation. It is particularly good for women, who are extra prone to grow more dependent rather than independent, and clearly a definite requirement for those who want to be married or a nun.

Because I'm one of the rare nuns who lives alone now and probably forever, living alone for a while is clearly one of the best things I'm doing before I die. For lifers, living alone gradually becomes one of life's greatest joys and freedoms. Not only are you able to do all ten things on this list whenever you want, you also don't have to worry about crumbs in the butter, or make the bed or do dishes until company comes. No small bonus.

---

[1]*The I Ching*, p. 91.

CONVENT BUTTER
↓

KAROL JACKOWSKI'S BUTTER
↓

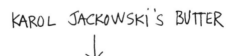

Ninth Thing:

Treat Yourself

When it comes to the care and feeding of your very best self there's no greater way to do both than by treating yourself. Be good to yourself. You learn to treat yourself when you live alone because chances are if you don't, no one else will. There's simply no one else around. No one to beg, "Honey, would you please go to the Dairy Queen and get me a banana split blizzard?"

Now for some, the care and feeding of one's very best self means lots of exercise, no meat, no fried foods, and no white sugar or flour. For others it means all of the above except exercise, plus never buying shoes you have to bend over to tie. Because I happen to be one of the others, the philosophy promoted here is not at all exclusive, except of that which becomes excessive and harmful to body and soul. Moderation in all things including moderation. That's the rule for treating yourself.

Why Treat Yourself?

Trying to be your very best self, day in and day out, during the best and worst of times is exceedingly, intensely, profoundly difficult, and no one knows more than you the greatness of the difficulty. For that reason alone you should treat yourself. Being your very best self always and forever, especially in the very worst of circumstances, takes such a powerful lot out of you that treating yourself becomes like manna from heaven. "I shall rain down bread for you from the heavens," said the Lord (Ex 16:4) — or chocolate malts from heaven, or soft-shell crabs from heaven, or fresh flowers in every room, or new foaming bath gels, or a trip to England in March. Even the gorilla suit you always wanted can be an extra divine prize from heaven.

Of course, if you have no desire to be your very best self now or forever, then there are likely to be no divinely inspired treats or prizes in store for you at all. Pity. Settling for less, you have already taken your reward and receive exactly what you've taken, no more, sometimes less, never surpassing the value of your effort or the purity of your intention.

Those nowhere near their best selves are the poorest, most chaotic, most pathetic selves around. Mistreating themselves, they are mistreated by others, and do the mistreating of others they do to themselves. Before long all the mistreating gets so big there's seemingly no way out. Those estranged from their very best selves and from God are doomed to mistreat (not treat) themselves and others forever, one of the absolute worst things to do before you die.

What Treats Do

The most important thing treats do is teach you how to treat others. "Always treat others as you would like them to treat you; that is the Law and the Prophets" (Mt 7:12). Or treat others the same way you treat yourself. All the same. By learning to care for and feed your very best self, you almost automatically learn how to care for and feed the very best selves of others. It's kind of magic, essentially religious, never merely philanthropic. Love of neighbor is inseparable from love of very best self and God. "Anyone who says 'I love God' and hates his neighbor, is a liar . . whoever loves God, must also love his neighbor" (1 Jn 4:20-21). Treating others the way you treat yourself is one of the biggest, most divine lessons treats teach you.

What all this treating looks like in real life can best be found in love of enemies, those within as well as without (Mt 5:43-47). It is pardon without limits for your very best self and others (Mt 18:21 ff), constant good given in return for constant evil now and forever (Rom 12:14-21). Treating yourself shines divine when it makes you patient, kind, not jealous, not snobbish, never rude, never self-seeking, never prone to anger nor brooding over injuries, not rejoicing over what is wrong but rejoicing with the truth. When treating is divine there's no limit to love's forbearance, to its trust, its hope, its power to endure (1 Cor 13:4-8)—no limit to all the everlasting treats. Nice.

The world is an awe-inspiring,
sacred, holy environment, in which
the forces of the unseen shine through
the visible environment
and in which terror and love,
Hate and favor, the Ghostly
and the demonic, the spirit world
and the shining glory of deities are
perceptible to the inward eye....

The WORLD provides the material
for Religious experience.

ANNE BANCROFT
(BUT NOT THE ANNE BANCROFT)

ORIGINS OF THE SACRED

So the treating of self and others means either a refreshing discovery of love that never fails or simply getting fat, spending a lot of money and having a so-so time. The divine beauty of a banana split blizzard is clearly in the eye (or in this case, the mouth) of the beholder where one's very best self, God and all other beauty lies. Treating yourself helps keep the eye calm, clear and cheerful so that the shine of the divine can be seen everywhere. That way, everything the eye beholds is a treat.

Tenth Thing:

Live Like You Have Nothing to Lose

Well now, if you've faithfully done things one through nine, the only thing literally left to do before you die is to live like you have nothing to lose. With all the digging, searching, listening, losing and finding that goes on with the first nine things, chances are all wits have been scared clean out of you and whatever there was to lose got lost. The first nine things to do before you die, while appearing innocent, fun and harmless, are at first try, real killers. Stuff like that is always better pointed out in the end.

Having done all nine, however, you've most likely faced your worst fears, had anguish camp out in your heart for years, and have probably seen your worst nightmares and hidden anxieties come to life before your very eyes. When all that's known is the losing side of having nothing to lose, ". . . we can only endure barely conscious, barely surviving the pain and powerlessness, suspended out of life, stuck, until and if, some act of grace with some new wisdom arrives."[1]

The effect of losing everything there is to lose is much like that of Ezekiel's vision of the dry bones, all broken and left scattered in little pieces, clearly with nada nada nada left to lose. The dark side of having nothing left to lose always lies in having to lose absolutely everything. And until all fear of loss is gone, there's always something left to lose. "In love there is no room for fear, but perfect love drives out all fear . . . whoever is afraid has not come to perfection in love" (1 Jn 4:18). Casting out all fear of loss is the meanest deadliest darkest part of having nothing to lose.

Well, thanks be to God for the cyclic movement of life: the waxing and waning of the moon, light succeeding darkness even as darkness overcomes the light, the eternal myth of death and resurrection. Having lost all that is not your very best self and God, what remains is mysteriously not dead but secretly alive. Regardless of how dead loss feels, life is clearly hidden somewhere in the deadest of times.

We all rise again like the moon. Our very best God makes us all rise again, but never the same as before. Always brand new. Losing everything there is to lose leaves us fearless, scareless, indestructible and brand new, ever virgin, capable of being assumed into heaven at any moment.

Even the ordinary manner of life becomes strangely, calmly different. No longer afraid, and with nothing to lose, life does not oppress, afflict, distress nor weary you as it did before. When loss becomes part of the hidden subtle divine movement of life instead of always someone else's fault, perspective

DRY BONES
HEAR THE WORD OF THE LORD!

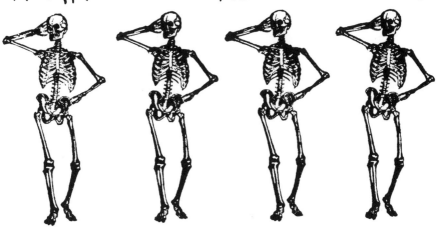

I WILL PUT BREATH IN YOU,
CAUSE FLESH TO COME UPON YOU,
COVER YOU WITH SKIN
AND YOU SHALL LIVE.

EZECHIEL 37:4-7

gets bigger and broader, and compassion is felt for all who suffer. In *Letters to a Young Poet*, philosopher and poet Rainer Maria Rilke believes such a renewal of the human spirit

> . . . will transform the love experience, which is now filled with error, will change it from the ground up, and reshape it into a relationship that is meant to be between one human being and another, no longer one that flows from man to woman. And this more human love (which will fulfill itself with infinite consideration and gentleness, and kindness and clarity in binding and releasing) will resemble what we are now preparing painfully and with great struggle: the love that consists in this: that two solitudes protect and border and greet one another.[2]

"Our bones are dry, our hope has gone; we are done for" no longer (Ez 37:11). Healing comes naturally, gradually, in its own time. Peace is God's gift then. The peace that passes any understanding. Eventually the dry bones get breath, flesh, skin, and come to life again. Then both "heart and body cry out for joy to the living God" (Ps 84:2). Then God's gifts are pure joy, simple delight, and certainly having more fun than anyone else. Joy that is at last complete. Clearly, there is none more free than one who has nothing to lose.

So now you see living with nothing to lose is the closest to divine you can get. Having lost all but your very best self and God, it's extra clear that being your best self has a divine effect on everything around. Life—all parts of life—gradually become noticeably more divine.

For John of the Cross, there is no greater or more necessary work than love. St. Augustine counsels

"Love and do what you will." Same thing. "God is love and those who abide in love abide in God and God in them" (cf. 1 Jn 4:16). And the more perfect the love, the more pure and complete the joy, which brings everyone back to the beginning—the fun part, having more fun than anyone else, the first and last thing to do before you die. Live like you have nothing to lose and have more fun than anyone else—the end and the beginning running into each other over and over and over again like some kind of eternal life. Which is exactly what these ten things aim to do for you before you die: show you how to undo death and live forever.

Not bad for $5.95.

---

[1]Sylvia Brinton Perera, *Descent to the Goddess*, Toronto: Inner City Books, 1981, p. 36.

[2]Rainer Maria Rilke, *Letters to a Young Poet*, Stephen Mitchell, trans., New York: Random House, 1984, p. 78.

JMJ

LOVE: THE "L" WORD

BY JOHN OF THE CROSS

Like the Bee that sucks Honey from all the wild flowers and will not use them for anything else, the soul easily extracts the sweetness of love from all the things that Happen to her, that is, she loves God thus everything leads her to love... And her pleasure in all things and in everything that happens is always the delight of loving (her very best self, work and) God.

Afterword

At this point in the "Ten Things to Do Before You Die" lecture, there was a demonstration of living like you have nothing to lose. Pointing out that the demonstration could indeed be the last thing I did before I died since that was hypothetically my last lecture, I also explained that no nun and dean at the age of 42 should ever do what I was about to do unless there was clearly nothing to lose. The students were given red hot cinnamon lips candy and the assignment to think through the list and pick their favorite thing to do before they die. I disappeared briefly to prepare for the finale.

Shortly after, I appeared from the balcony and finished the lecture in a gorilla suit—something I've always wanted to do. While a good time was clearly had by all, certainly I had more fun than anyone else. As you may have guessed, Having More Fun Than Anyone Else, Finding a Place to Escape Reality, and Treating Yourself were top favorites among the students. While Thinking About Becoming a Nun was clearly not, all admitted it was far more interesting than they ever thought possible. The other items were too hard and way too serious to think about on a starry spring night. While recognized as absolutely necessary and commendable, the remaining items received polite but not wildly enthusiastic applause.

With regard to the entire list of "Ten Things to Do Before You Die," all are advised to begin with number one and work through all ten, omitting none. That way you're sure to keep ending up at the beginning, never stopping dead, which is the biggest bonanza surprise of all. Those dry broken bones come to life over and over and over, indestructible. Unable to die, you just keep getting better and better at being your very best self, becoming more and more divine, assumed more and more into heaven. Or you can just assume that's heaven. Whatever.

"The new time has arrived and with it good fortune. And just as the sun shines forth in redoubled beauty after rain, or as a forest grows more freshly green from charred ruins after a fire, so the new era appears all the more glorious by contrast with the misery of the old."[1]

Which means, once upon a time there lived a girl who had more fun than anyone else, got some insight, got some depth, found a place to escape reality, wrote something at the end of every day, thought about being a nun, made herself interesting, lived alone for a while, treated herself, and lived like she had nothing to lose—she did all ten things before she died and lived happily ever after.

For $5.95 you even get a fairy tale ending.

---

[1] *I Ching*, p. 251